Business Tips for Creative People

SIMPLICITIES OF BIRTHING

YOUR VISION **Tanya Yvonne**

Business Tips for Creative People

Copyright © 2018 by **Tanya Yvonne**. All Rights Reserved.

All rights reserved. No part of this publication may be reproduced, transmitted, or stored in a retrieval system, in any form or by any means, electronic, mechanical, photocopying, recording or otherwise, without the prior permission of the author. This book is sold subject to the condition that it shall not, by way of trade or otherwise, be lent, re-sold, hired or otherwise circulated without the author's prior consent in any form of binding other than that in which it is published, and without a similar condition including this condition being imposed on the subsequent purchaser.

TABLE OF CONTENTS

Dedications.. v

Acknowledgments vii

Introduction ix

Tips..1

Chapter One: It's Not About Me..............................19

Chapter Two: Nothing In Life Is Free... Yes, It Is!.....23

Chapter Three: The Journey... 29

Chapter Four: "Praise God.......................................35

Business Resources 39

Biography 42

DEDICATIONS

To my Granny and Granddad (rih). If it wasn't for you two loving me, teaching me, and giving me the tools to live life, I don't know where I would be. Thank you for taking me in when I was a young, angry, wild child who didn't have a clue. You both taught me how to love myself, pay bills, build credit, not to trust boys, and be aware that not everyone is your friend. You were always there when I needed you the most.

Thanks, Granny, for reading the Word of God to me when I was young, and allowing me to read the Word to you. You always told me how smart I was, even when I didn't want to be. Thank you Granddad (rih) for instilling in me how important tithing was, and telling everyone, "Tanya, Go be Alright!" I Love you both more than you could ever know. I just wanted to make you both proud. And, Granddad, I hope you're looking down smiling and saying, "She got it."

To my children, Sarquese and TreTaurian, you both are my blessings from God, my backbones, my loves, my heartbeats. Sarquese, thank you for being so mature and understanding. Thank you both for loving me in all my mess. Thank you Sarquese for your support and the encouraging words you give to me. Thank you TreTaurian for teaching me what unconditional love is, and how to be patient. Thank you both for always taking care of your mom, no matter what. You both inspire me to do better. I thank God for breaking the generational curses off of you two. Only He knows all the love I have for you both. Thank you for being my children, and I'm so grateful to be your mom.

ACKNOWLEDGMENTS

Thank you Bishop Ben Gibert (rih), for allowing God to use you to teach me the Word of God. I didn't understand it until I came to your church. You have planted many seeds and led by example being a husband, father, spiritual father, and leader. I am very blessed to have been under you and Dr. C's Ministry. I'm walking in my destiny, thank you RIH.

Katrina Mitchell, I love you. I remember the day you told me I was going to write a book, not one but two. I didn't have a clue! I responded, "I'm not a writer." But the Holy Spirit knew, so thank you for allowing Him to use you in more ways than you will ever know. Thank you for believing in me when I didn't believe in myself.

Darlene Dickson, you are amazing! I thank you for watering the seeds that were planted. I thank you for your creativity and for sharing your knowledge that blessed me to become a writer and author. I thank you for your patience, and for allowing me to open up, write and express myself.

INTRODUCTION

It is a lot easier to start your own business than you think. Whether it's hair braiding, doing massages, making tee shirts, baking cookies, cakes or teaching people how to get their finances in order, all you need is an idea or a dream; then step out there on some faith.

There are simple ways to start up—business cards, flyers, social media or word of mouth (networking); whichever you choose, it can and will be a success. It all depends on how much you trust God, and believe in yourself and your dreams. Hey, Dream BIG! The more you believe in yourself and your dreams, the more everyone else will also. There is an entrepreneurial spirit in everyone. Everyone as an adult, teen, and even child has sold something, thought about selling something, or even made something to sell.

Everyone has come up with a brilliant idea and wants someone to support it. Most times, people can find someone to support their idea.

Every adult, either man or woman, shall at least have one or two businesses of their own. God, our creator, has created us to create, multiply and be fruitful. The more business owners there are the less poverty, homelessness, and crime. No one will have time to focus on what they don't have because everyone will be busy creating and birthing out their dreams and visions.

As for me, I did not know I was called to be an entrepreneur. I just wanted to make tee shirts with these witty expressions that the Lord downloaded in me over a period, wearing them all without anyone knowing where they had come from. But God had another plan. I was told by my Spiritual Mother that this gift was not mine to keep; I had to share and bless others with it.

Today, I must say, along with others, "My tees are a blessing to others." IT IS NOT ABOUT ME! Once you start, you too will begin to realize your gifts and talents are not really about you either. God just used you to carry them, birth them, then bless people with them, as He does with our natural children.

In a simple form, God uses you to be a blessing to others, but you are the one who gets compensated for it (make sense?). The closer you get to your destiny, the harder the fight becomes. You must stay focused and prayed up; if not, you may get distracted, and it may take a little longer than planned.

Fear, lack of confidence, lack of resources and finances are some of the excuses why people do not move forward with their business ventures. Me, I was a little different. I wanted to try every business idea I thought of. And I did! When it took off and was a success that was when the spirit of fear and negative thoughts would come. I would then tell myself why I couldn't continue. Sounds crazy, right? I know! Yes, it has taken me a while to get here.

Only because of me! No one else. It is what you allow. So, don't become your own worst enemy. And do not join your haters' clique!

Become your number one cheerleader. Buy pompoms, a whistle, a bullhorn and say your cheers (prayers and affirmations) EVERY DAY! Then SING THEM (your worship songs) to keep you going and in the mood.

How can we cheer other people on but not ourselves? I struggled with that for years. That is why it's so easy for me to assist others, and write this book. I can honestly say it was very easy to build the foundation and find all the resources needed to start all my business ventures. It doesn't seem like it—remember it was my fault! That is why I just give so much FREE information away. I help and assist because the Lord blessed and favored me through this whole process with resources, information, people, and vendors. I'm blessed to be a blessing, and besides, God loves a cheerful giver. It is just in my heart to do so. Why hold on to information? If you got it, give it; assist, help and be the woman or man of God the Lord has called you to be.

There are some things you may run into starting your business or tapping into your creative side; for instance, some people will not like you or what you are doing. You will begin to realize who is really for you, and who the haters are. Trust me! You will have some, and it may even hurt a little. I was in denial for a couple of years. The truth is, if they're not being productive or trying to do something positive, it will create issues. They will hate with their heart but not with their mouth if you know what I mean. Some people would rather support strangers than you. Some will judge, some will hope you don't succeed, and some will just boldly be jealous. Just stay focused and prayed up. Once again, ask God for wisdom, favor, humility, grace, discernment, and patience, and through this process, it shall be given unto you in Jesus' name.

~Taan

I dedicate this to my children

Sarquese and TreTaurian and

grandparents Orzer and Wanna Spencer.

Special thanks to Katrina Michele

Mitchell for planting the seed and Darlene Dickson for watering the seed until it blossomed.

-TIPS-

1. BE STILL

Psalms 46:10 KJV. Be still and know that I am God:

Being still, in meditating, is an awesome thing to do. It allows you to quiet your spirit man to hear from God. He speaks to you about everything. We think about things to do that we need to do or have done, and just thank God in the midst. It is your time with Him and the Holy Spirit together. It's peaceful to be still; God will give you visions and ideas, along with the blueprint you need to get there.

The more time you spend with God, the more revelation and confirmation you will receive about your destiny.

2. PRAY

Mark 11:24 KJV. Therefore, I say unto you, what things whosoever ye desire, when ye pray, believe that ye received them and ye shall have them.

Prayer is the best thing I can do for myself and anybody. I have seen things really happen when prayer takes place. Deliverance, healing, breakthroughs, restoration, you name it.

God will give you the desires of your heart if you are obedient to His call. Praying and prayer should be a part of everyone's daily life. Without it, I would not be who I am today, and neither would my children. Prayer at church, prayer calls or prayer groups are also great ways to commune with God. But make sure to pray; it doesn't matter where you are, in your car, shower, outside, anywhere! Stay prayed up!

3. BE OBEDIENT

1 Samuel 15:22 KJV. And Samuel said, Hath the Lord as great delight in burnt offerings and sacrifices, as in obeying the voice of the Lord?

Behold, to obey is better than sacrifice, and to hearken than the fat of rams...

I can go on and on about obedience.

It keeps me out of trouble, and helps me focus on what I am supposed to be doing. When you're obedient to "thus said the Lord," things shift, favor will follow you, and peace would be upon you. There are so many blessings that come with obedience. Our Father loves it when we listen to Him, just as we love it when our children listen and obey us. God knows our beginning, our middle and our end. He wants the very best for us. So why not be obedient? It's not the easiest thing to do in the beginning, but fearing and trusting in the Lord has a lot to do with obedience. It is very important when it comes to making choices; your life depends on it.

Disobedience allows major distractions to take place. I know because I've been there. A thing that could have taken a week may take a year because of disobedience. So much for that. It's all about being obedient so you can receive your full blessing.

4. JOURNAL EVERY THOUGHT AND IDEA

Habakkuk 2:2 KJV. And the Lord answered me, and said, Write the vision, and make it plain upon tables, that he may run that readeth it.

Freelance writing or journaling is a therapy and an outlet for many. I've noticed at times when I write what the Lord spoke after a day of meditation or what I want to accomplish comes to pass. But it all depends on me and the distractions I allow to take place. It feels awesome to go back months or years later to see what I accomplished on the list. Also, after writing, going back to take a look at how far you've come, spirituality, emotionally, financially, and mentally. I never thought I could write a book, but journaling is a book before it has been edited.

I used to carry a small pocket tablet just to write any little idea or expression I thought of, then I would go back and take a look at what was written. Having things documented is everything. I thank God for the scripture on this. It truly blesses. Try it; you'll be amazed at what you get out of it—a business, a book, a plan, a successful future, discipline, structure, and responsibility.

5. ALLOW GOD TO LEAD YOU

Psalms 23 KJV (the entire chapter)

When listening to God and allowing Him to lead you in everything, you can't go wrong in any way. This psalm has gotten me through a lot, and I still say it aloud quite often. It has everything in it concerning everyday life. Ask God; He will answer, and He will show up and show out for you. All He wants to know is "It's His will, not yours." The Lord has led me out of a mess that I never thought I could get out of. On the other side, He has led me to great things that were a blessing to my life and my children's lives. You have to trust Him that He will, and can, make crooked paths straight.

6. STAY CONNECTED TO YOUR SPIRITUAL FAMILY

Matt 18:20 KJV. For where two or three are gathered together in my name, there am I in the midst of them

To have a spiritual family that is praying with you and for you is a blessing. You can feel its covering. There are things against you—such as the world, the devil and yourself—and you need someone to come in to intercede on your behalf. I have an awesome spiritual family including my spiritual mothers, sisters, and brothers.

My spiritual father passed away in February 2017, and it seemed the covering had been removed. For months, I felt lost and a little weary. I didn't want to continue the plan God had for me, even though someone was praying for me but I wasn't able to pray for myself. I was distracted by things of the world. I had no interest in writing, making tees or school at the time. The wonderful thing about being connected in the spirit with people who love you and are obedient is that they will call you and tell you, "Thus said the Lord," even if you don't want to hear it. Also, much prayer would be going forth.

Once again God will send the right people at the right time while you're on your journey to make sure you reach your destiny. First, pray, seek the Lord and ask if that person is supposed to be there. The same way God sends His people and angels, the adversary sends his people and demons too. Be careful; ask for wisdom and discernment, and it will be given to you.

7. STAY AWAY FROM THE HATERS

Luke 6:28 KJV. Bless them that curse you, and pray for them that despitefully use you.

Everyone involved in something positive has haters. They could be family, friends, coworkers, people who don't know you, and even some church folks! Yes, I said it! Some may pretend to be on your side, but they're not. Proverbs 26:25. Then you may have some who downright hate you for no reason, but honestly, that's not your battle; it's the Lord's, vengeance is His.

Deuteronomy 32:35. Just beware of the haters. Stay focused, and don't let everyone know what you're doing.

Just do it! I was amazed at the people who had problems with my businesses and what I was doing. Family and friends! It was a huge shock to me. It hurt a lot to know their feelings and some of their actions. When I got over the emotional struggle, I began to feel stronger but kept my mouth shut in regards to my business plans.

I prayed more specifically to keep myself, my finances, and my vision covered until they came to pass. After knowing someone closest to you is not for you, that's when you realize your destiny is at stake. Keep walking, stand firm, and still love them, some from afar, but love them anyway.

8. BE FREE

John 8:36 KJV. If the Son therefore, shall make you free, ye shall be free indeed.

You have to have some freedom in being creative. It is your outlet, which means you can do whatever you want to do. Own it and do what your heart desires to. Knowing who you are in Christ is freedom all by itself!

9. CREATIVITY HAS NO BOUNDARIES

Proverbs 18:16 KJV. A man's gift maketh room for him and bring him before great men.

Our gifts and talents will get attention from people, and make room for our life without any boundaries. When people ask me my opinions when it comes to their home or tees, I tell them, "It's not what I want or think, it's whatever you like and want to do." People will conform to your masterpieces. The sky is the limit, so don't worry about rules, regulations or directions from anyone concerning what God has told you to do.

Everything created has come from Him and Him alone. God had no boundaries when He created the earth and things on the earth. So when it comes to creativity and God's children, we have no boundaries either. Walk in your purpose, we all have one and fulfill your vision.

You never know who may need your services, products or words of wisdom.

10. A MANUAL IS NOT - NEEDED

Psalms 90:17 KJV. And let the Beauty of the Lord our God Be upon us: and establish thou the works of our hands upon us; yea, the work of our hands established thou it.

No one but God can confirm the work that you do, not man! If the Lord told you to go ahead, it is done, and something else needs to be added then do so. There is no book to tell you what to create and give you your vision, dream or idea but GOD! I know I keep repeating that, but it's the truth. Yes, I have read articles, had a mentor, and listen to motivational speakers after I had started.

I'm not saying you shouldn't become knowledgeable about your business or your business idea. I'm only saying a book cannot download in you your creative purpose.

Only the good book can—the Bible. The more you read God's Word, the more He will speak to you about everything that concerns you—church, ministry, family, finances, relationships, education, and business. Just trust God with it all.

11. SOMEONE WILL BE - INSPIRED

Psalms 112:2, 3, 5, 6

2) His seed shall be mighty upon the earth: the generation of the upright shall be blessed. 3) Wealth and riches shall be in his house. 5)A good man sheweth favor and lendeth: He will guide his affairs with discretion. 6) Surely, he shall not be moved forever: the righteous shall be in everlasting remembrance

Mark 16:20 KJV. And they went forth, and preached everywhere, the Lord working with them, and confirming the word with signs following. Amen

It is because of whose you are, you are favored. Anything that comes from the Lord has to prosper. You being a man or woman in Him gives you godly characteristics: a tither, sower, cheerful giver, honest, kind, diligent; I could keep going. When people know your character, they want to sow into you because it is you.

Your business is a ministry; you may not see it with that perspective now, but it is. You're providing a service or product that someone needs, and that is a blessing. Your spirit will minister to them; you being kind, you giving a discount, saying encouraging words is a ministry. Your customers will then tell someone; then they will tell someone else. Once again, because of whose you are, and what you're giving, and I'm not talking about your product or services. I'm speaking of the God that dwells in you, and what He has called you to do. People will see and know that they're sowing into good ground and would be blessed. You're providing, but it's more than your creations—know that!

TANYA YVONNE

CHAPTER ONE

IT'S NOT ABOUT ME

Psalms 46:10- Be still and know that I am God

In the midst of your storm, God speaks and begins to show you your gifts and talents. I would leave my beautiful home that was toxic and chaotic, and go to a place I called Peace.

A place with water, ducks, and trees. There I was always able to sit still, talk to God, cry to God, and listen to Him. Then I would pray silently while looking at the pond. Sometimes my eyes were shut. I would go there quite often to sit and wait to hear Him speak!

Early in the morning, God began speaking to me, telling me little corky things, thoughts and expressions repeatedly. Nights and nights went by; then He told me to write them down. I then kept a journal on my nightstand so that when I heard that small still voice, I would begin to write down everything He had spoken. It became a routine that I enjoyed, not only the Lord speaking to me, but the intimacy we began to share. I did not understand any of this, but I was obedient.

Be obedient: 1 Samuel 15:22 KJV. Do it afraid; God will do the rest.

Stepping out on faith can be a little uncomfortable. But allow the Holy Spirit to lead you, and keep your eye on the prize. You will be led to do things in the physical realm that you had to do in the spirit realm. Once again, walk by faith, not by sight (2 Corinthians 5:7) and listen! Everything will fall into place. Doors will open; resources will come about.

I did not have a clue about starting a business; I just wanted to make tee shirts and wear them all myself. I wasn't thinking about anyone else wearing them; I did not want anyone else wearing them. I just figured

I would wear a different one every day for at least 100 days, depending on my mood.

As I began to birth my tees, with the help of my creative cousin Brandon, owner and operator of Reality Designs, I noticed it was not as hard as I'd imagined; actually, it was easy. I created four tees. Yes, I wore the first one and boy did I get complimented on it. At first, I was too afraid to let anyone know I was the creator until Ms. Kesha asked me, "Yeah Tanya, I love that tee shirt, too. Where did you get it?"

I then told her, "I created it!"

She stopped and said, "You did that?"

I said, "Yes!"

Another lady asked me, "Are you selling?"

I said, "No."

Ms. Kesha said, "I want to buy a couple anyway." Still in my mind, I had no intentions of selling.

The conversation then got around to me! I began to show them the other tees. Ms. Kesha said, "You are sitting on a million-dollar idea." I still wasn't convinced, but I did make and sell a couple of tee shirts at a price between 20 and 25 dollars. I still did not see the vision. In the back of my mind, I did not want anyone wearing my shirts. I then created a fifth shirt...

My Spiritual Mom loved it. I told her, "I don't want to sell my tees; I just want to wear them."

She began to tell me this was not about me, and how many people would be blessed. She went on and on, then prayed with me. I began to obey God. My tees were not about me; GOD just used me to get the message out!

That's it!

CHAPTER TWO

NOTHING IN LIFE IS FREE... YES, IT IS!

2 Cor 9:8-11- God can make all grace abound to you

After my separation and moving out of my second home, I had to move back in with my grandparents, where I grew up. Boy was that hard.

My son stayed with my ex-husband at the time, and that took a toll on me. I felt like a teenager all over again. Moving from a four-bedroom house with 2 full baths, full basement, party deck, private fence and 2.5 car garage to a small bedroom full of everyone else's things was very humbling. I felt like my life was an open book now, and it couldn't get any worse than this.

Going through a divorce, a bankruptcy, in school, serving at Unity Cathedral of Faith, and between congregations, I just didn't understand my life at the time. But GOD! He began speaking again about things I had no clue about. One thing He did say was that I was not to discuss what He was about to do with anybody. Once again, I was obedient. He began to show me how to start my tee shirt business, and where to go to do so. It was a smooth journey. Doors opened, and the favor was given. It was like God was telling me every step to take and honestly, I came out of $151 for

EVERYTHING.

At the time, this was my first DBA—doing business as a DBA is making sure no one else has your business name, and if not, you get it registered and it is good for five years. It used to be free, now it's $16, which is still not a bad price. As soon as I received my DBA, I called the Michigan Treasury Department from the city clerk's office and received my sales tax ID number. Yes, you can do it over the phone or online, whichever way is convenient for you. It is also called

An Employer Identification Number (EIN), and it is free. You need your EIN for tax purposes.

My cousin and I created my logo, which was pretty easy. I found one part of it from Vistaprint, and my font came from the internet. My business cards were made for $50 because I wanted a high gloss. Although I purchased my thank you cards from Vistaprint for free, I had to pay for shipping. My Michigan trademark was $50 as well. My logo was trademarked because I did not want anyone trying to take what I had done. Also, if you have art work in your logo, you can get that copy written, which is $35. Copywrite doesn't do text only, trademark does. You can print your application online and send it in with a check or money order. Be sure to follow the directions before sending in.

An LLC is a Limited Liability

Corporation. This protects you as an individual, and consumers can only go after your business. Resources can be found at the back of this book.

I was like, "That's it, God!" What was I afraid of? All I could think of was the unknown, but the unknown was an awesome experience. I felt like a pro, like, "This is it!" It seemed like a cake walk, but I know it was nothing but God's grace. He put people in my life who wanted to genuinely help and teach me the business; things that were priceless. Designers were teaching me how to design and create my style and brand of apparel. Boutique owners were talking to me about putting my tees in their store when they were printed, and also about the business itself. Now, mind you, I did not personally know any of these people. Not only was I inspired to do tees, but also to design clothes and then have my boutique one day. The seeds were planted.

I was doing homework, drawing, writing, praying, reading and crying. I was drawing pictures of jeans I wanted to make and DID. They were sharp; I got a lot of compliments on them. I couldn't believe I DID THAT! I started writing down everything I wanted to accomplish along with scripture, or just scriptures alone, for encouragement. I remember Pastor Haddon praying for me, telling me to write my vision, and make it plain, that restoration was about to take place.

That has been with me ever since, and I am still writing. For me, it feels good to go back to my writings and see everything I have accomplished from my list and see where God has brought me from and out of. Speaking of God bringing me out, sometimes we just need a little deliverance in some areas of our life, so that we can move on. When you have people in your life who care about your soul and spirit, that's priceless.

TANYA YVONNE

CHAPTER THREE

THE JOURNEY...

Joshua 1:9- "Have not I commanded thee? Be strong and of good courage; be not afraid, neither be thou dismayed: for the Lord thy God is with thee whithersoever thou goest."

Joshua 1:9 is one of the scriptures my spiritual mom came to my house with for Bible study. I did not know what to do with it. I'd heard it, and we discussed it, but I was still confused and afraid. I thought it went into one ear and out of the other. That was how it seemed at the time. I allowed many things to distract me because I was afraid to face my gifts, talents, and creativity. Although when I did anything about it, everything came naturally. When you're dealing with a lot of baggage, as I was, that can be the biggest hindrance of them all! You cannot see clearly or focus on what God has called you to do.

I wanted to know what my purpose was, but I didn't want to go through the process. All I could remember was hurt, pain, anger, hate, etc. I lived my life that way and didn't even know it. Many times, God will open doors and give you opportunities that will intimidate you. You may miss your blessing because of fear, without knowing God did it. You have to rebuke fear, procrastination, inadequacy and many more negative spirits that will entangle you and prevent you from birthing your destiny. When the devil knows that God has a plan for you, he will try his best to get you off track with all kinds of things if you allow him to.

First of all, I did not think my tee shirts were great, so I didn't advertise or market them as I should've. My family and friends were my biggest support along with a lot of people they knew. I guess you could say I didn't take my tee shirt business as seriously as I should have done. Also, my name, ChayilCreazions, it really wasn't me; I was kind of ashamed or embarrassed to say it. I don't know why but I was.

"Just Taan T's," there's so much freedom there! God dropped even more expressions after the name change. My tees were even different; they represented me more—Tanya Yvonne!

My business coach is the best. She walked me through everything I needed her to and more.

She was always available to truthfully answer any questions I had.

I felt as though she wanted my business to prosper more than I did. That is what you need, people on your team who see your vision, and who can also help you birth it with no hatred. Yes, everyone who is thinking about becoming an entrepreneur needs a coach or mentor. Today, I meditate on that scripture and many more. That is what got me through, and to the next step.

I always wondered how it was possible to come up with all these brilliant business ideas, being shown exactly how they were to be; BUT keeping them going, and even completing some was a struggle. Until one day, my Spiritual mother, Mother Womack, wrote me a beautiful letter along with a card. The letter said how creative, gifted and talented I was, but I also had broken relationships in my family that caused me heartache, pain, and unforgiveness. She stated that once I was completely healed, my business would prosper.

As time went on, I started to believe that. It was like I was starting a lot of things, but they were not going as planned from my tees to Queens to my home care company. I was determined to get everything complete, but I was all over the place. Even in completing this little book, it felt like forever doing so. As time went on, God was healing, purging and breaking stuff off me, and delivered me at the same time. Money was tight, and some people weren't right! I had to keep going with brokenness, demons, confusion and all! I was determined to kick the devil butt!

One day, I was sitting back thinking about my whole life. As I thought about how strong I was physically and mentally, I wondered why God wouldn't make me strong spiritually. Everything starts first in the spirit realm…. so, if I'm strong in those other areas, I have to be spiritually strong first! Thus said the Lord. I had finally got it and tapped into it! God was the beginning and head of everything! I had to ask Him first. He would tell me, "You need to listen to Me and be obedient about everything!" That included business—who to work with, who not to work with, what to buy, when to buy, and what to give. It became easier; I allowed God to be in control of this entire journey. Your business is your ministry.

TANYA YVONNE

CHAPTER FOUR

"PRAISE GOD...

Psalms 145- Exalt You, my God the king and praise your name forever and ever.

Prophecy is an awesome thing... My prophecies are still coming to pass as I am writing this book. I thank God so much for life! For an abundant life! I see my children, what they're doing, and where I am at now. It took me months to get to this last chapter because I am still in the process of completing things including school, businesses, relationships and myself. What I've learned throughout this journey is that when your heart desires a thing or things, they become easy to obtain.

Stay focused and diligent. I now love me and know my worth, all of my businesses' worth, and what I've been created here to do.

Your business is your story; your business is your passion; your business is your love; your business is you. Handle it with care, please! So many doors can and will open for you when you're willing to give yourself the credit you deserve to walk through and boldly know that there is just one of you.

No one has the same thing. I do tee shirts, right? A lot of people do tee shirts. But no one has the expressions I have, and I don't have what others have! I design clothes; there are so many awesome designers out there who make some of the best pieces I have seen, purchased and still want, but yet, still, we do not have the same thing. That is what makes us all a unique brand. We may do the same thing, but not the same way.

So, Do You and Be You to the Fullest! Why wait until… Until what or until when? I know you heard, "Do It Afraid!"

I love Joyce Meyer. If you are struggling with the inner man, just know also that's not the real you, the real you is the one to whom God gave the idea, gift, talent, and creativity. So, talk to that thing. When it says, "No, you can't," laugh and say, "Yes, I can and I will!" I had to learn to do that, and it worked.

The adversary does not want you to be a blessing to anybody, that is why he tells you those lies to keep you in bondage and hindered in moving forward to what God has planned for your life. We all have a destiny; it is up to us to stay humble, obedient and thank God for the process of getting there. You are closer than you think you are, just take move forward no matter what. I love to write down all of my accomplishments, and from where I've started.

Never look at where you're at, always stay focused on where you want to be, this will keep you positive, rich and feeling blessed at all times. As for me, staying focused means separating yourself from the world. Only allow who God wants in that space at the time. I do believe in divine connections and encounters.

Speaking of blessings, a close friend of mine shared a couple of things with me regarding her upbringing, which was a lot like mine—abuse, neglect, abandonment, you name it. She started doing research and received so much revelation from where it all came from to why it all happened. Now, mind you, about a year prior, the Lord spoke to me about sharing my story with the world for my freedom. He gave me a name and explained how everything was going to be in place.

I did a couple of videos regarding my past and present life, which has given me so much freedom. I love, love, love everything about it—the topics, the freedom, and the blessings. My motto is, "Tell the truth, shame the devil," and that's what is done on every taping. I thank God every day for all the blessings because just waking up is the biggest blessing of them all, then we have the freedom of making choices God's way or our own. We can go either way, but God's way is better than ours on any day. It's the little things that mean so much. Material things don't mean anything if you don't embrace God's love, family, friends, and service.

My life today, I love what I do and who I've become. As I continue to grow in the Lord, He will continue to bless me, my children, and their children's children. I am forever grateful that my God chose me to minister through my creativity from past hurts, pain, flaws and all.

BUSINESS RESOURCES

The Holy Bible King James Version

Book editing, publishing, and lectures: darlene@mgph.org

Business coaching: Katrina Mitchell Creative, www.katrinamichele.com

DBA (doing business as) … County-City Building

Employer ID Number (EIN)… States

Treasury Department

Evoice: Business

Telecommunications

Fiverr.com- marketing resources

Free business resources, legal advice, mentors, marketing, web design: Score.org

GoDaddy.com: Domain, website builder and hosting
Hiremymom.com - virtual assistance

HostGator.com: Hosting, Domain websites

iComputer.biz: For all your computer needs—soft/hardware purchase and repair

Personal budgeting and Finance advising: nje@normajeanevans.com

QUEENtrepreneurs: Networking B2B W2W - queentrepreneurs@gmail.com

Shopify: ecommerce website builder

Small business startup: sba.gov

TradeMark/Patent/Copywrite: USPTO.gov

Torealitydesigns@gmail.com:

Graphic designs, tee shirts, business cards flyers etc.

The Fashion Statement: Fashion

event production and promotional

modeling. Tfsservices1@gmail.com 929-266-6575

The Shirtery tee shirt shop: theshirtery.net

BUSINESS TIPS FOR CREATIVE PEOPLE

TeeSpring.com: For all your tee shirt needs

United Sonz Business Solutions: Tee shirts, business cards, flyers, silk screen & more - www.printingplusshirts.com

Vistaprint: Marketing resources

Versatrans: Custom transfers and custom vinyl for tees - www.versatranz.com

Wix.com: Free website building

BIOGRAPHY

Tanya Yvonne, born on the 22nd of April is from the Detroit Metropolitan Area. She's a divorcee and a mother of two young adults which she loves spending time with along with her godchildren, friends and some family.

Although she didn't have a great time in high school, Taan has a Bachelor of Science degree in Community Development with a minor in Psychology and She's now expecting to complete her Masters in Psychology by the end of 2021. She is excellent at multitasking which is evident in her being a teacher in the day and a T-shirt designer by night.

On the road to attaining financial freedom, she embarked on this mission to begin her own start-up. This became the basis of her first-ever book which is about the journey to entrepreneurship selling tees through the good, the bad and, the ugly along with bible scriptures as tips. Tanya aspires to be the best version of herself which would ultimately bring her peace and joy.

Tanya is an ambivert who gets along well with people. Lover of rest, seafronts, roller skating, and enjoys makes exciting podcasts.

www.ingramcontent.com/pod-product-compliance
Lightning Source LLC
Chambersburg PA
CBHW031549210526
45464CB00003B/1222